Oldham Surname

Ireland: 1600s to 1900s

From Ireland Church Records of Baptism, Marriage and Death

Comprised of Roman Catholic and Church of Ireland Records

From Counties Carlow, Cork, Kerry and Dublin City

Compiled by **Donovan Hurst**

March 10, 2013

ISBN: 1939958075
ISBN-13: 978-1-939958-07-5

Dedication

This work is dedicated to all of those that came before us and shaped our lives to make us the people that we are today.

Table of Contents

Introduction

This is a compilation of individuals who have the surname of Oldham that lived in the country of Ireland from the 1600s to the 1900s. I have placed each entry into one of four categories: Families, Individual Births/Baptisms, Individual Burials, and Individual Marriages. If a marriage entry primarily concerns an Individual Oldham whom is female, then I have placed that entry under the category of Individual Marriages. If a marriage entry primarily concerns an Individual Oldham whom is male, then I have placed that entry under the category of Families. Images of many of these listings are available at http://churchrecords.irishgenealogy.ie/churchrecords/.

To help guide the reader of this work, the format of this book is as follows:

- Main Family Entry (Husband and Wife) (Father and Mother)

  o Child of Main Family Entry, including Spouse(s) when available

    ▪ Grandchild of Main Family Entry, including Spouse(s) when available

      • Great-Grandchild of Main Family Entry, including Spouse(s) when available

(**Bolded Text**) following any entry includes any additional information such as Residence(s), Occupation(s), Signature(s), etc. when available.

Hurst

Some of the fonts used in this work symbolizes Celtic writing. The traditional letters, numbers, and punctuation marks and their Celtic counterparts are as follows:

Traditional Letters (Uppercase & Lowercase)

A a B b C c D d E f G g H I i J j K k L l M m N n O o P p Q q R r S s T t U u V v W w X x Y y Z z

Celtic Letters (Uppercase & Lowercase)

A a B b C c D ð E e F ƒ G g H h I i J j K k L l M m

N n O o P p Q q R ʀ S s T t U u V ʋ W ω X x Y ʏ Z z

Traditional Numbers

1 2 3 4 5 6 7 8 9 10

Celtic Numbers

1 2 3 4 5 6 7 8 9 10

Traditional Punctuation

. , : ' " & - ( )

Celtic Punctuation

. , : ' " & - ( )

Parish Churches

Cork & Ross

(Roman Catholic or RC)

Bandon Parish, Bantry Parish, Cork - South Parish, Ivelearly Parish, Kilbrittain Parish, Kilmichael Parish, Kilmurry Parish, and Murragh & Templemartin Parish.

Dublin (Church of Ireland)

Leeson Park Parish , Rathmines Parish, Rotunda Chapel Parish, St. Andrew Parish, St. Anne Parish, St. Audoen Parish, St. Bride Parish, St. George Parish, St. James Parish, St. Mark Parish, St. Mary Parish, St. Matthias Parish, St. Michan Parish, St. Nicholas Without Parish, St. Paul Parish, St. Peter Parish, St. Stephen Parish, St. Thomas Parish, St. Werburgh Parish, and Taney Parish.

Dublin (Roman Catholic or RC)

Lucan Parish, Palmerstown Parish, Rathfarnham Parish, Rathmines Parish, SS. Michael & John Parish, St. Andrew Parish, St. Audoen Parish, St. James Parish, St. Lawrence Parish, St. Mary, Haddington Road Parish, St. Mary, Pro Cathedral Parish, St. Michan Parish, and St. Nicholas Parish.

Hurst

Families

- Boland Oldham & Jane Donovan

  - Leonora Oldham – b. 27 Jul 1880, bapt. 2 Aug 1880 (Baptism, **Rathmines Parish** (RC))

Boland Oldham (father):

Residence - Mt. Pleasant Avenue - August 2, 1880

- Daniel Oldham & Mary Croneen – 24 Feb 1835 (Marriage, **Bantry Parish** (RC))

Wedding Witnesses:

Cornelius Croneen & Michael Croneen

- Ebenezer Oldham & Anne Oldham

  - Charles Oldham – bapt. 12 Dec 1819 (Baptism, **St. Mary Parish**)

- Edward Oldham & Mary Unknown

  - Edward Oldham – b. 1819, bapt. 1819 (Baptism, **Rathfarnham Parish** (RC))

- Frederick Oldham & Unknown

  - Thomas Oldham & Leonie Gaudon – 1 Oct 1848 (Marriage, **St. Mary Parish**)

Signatures:

Hurst

▪ Charles Thomas Oldham – b. 29 Jan 1849, bapt. 18 Feb 1849 (Baptism, **St. Peter Parish**)

Thomas Oldham (son):

   Residence - 1 Granby Place - October 1, 1848

      No. 9 Holles Row - February 18, 1849

   Occupation - Mercantile Clerk - October 1, 1848

      Servant - February 18, 1849

Leonie Gaudon, daughter of Simon Gaudon (daughter-in-law):

   Residence - 1 Granby Place - October 1, 1848

   Occupation - Dress Maker - October 1, 1848

Simon Gaudon (father):

   Occupation - Builder

Frederick Oldham (father):

   Occupation - Engineer

Wedding Witnesses:

George Cooke & Margaret Doyle

Signatures:

Oldham Surname Ireland: 1600s to 1900s

- George Oldham & Bridget Cullen

  - Emily Mary Oldham – b. 1 Aug 1878, bapt. 14 Aug 1878 (Baptism, **St. Lawrence Parish** (RC))

  - Louise Mary Oldham – b. 25 Jul 1880, bapt. 2 Aug 1880 (Baptism, **St. Lawrence Parish** (RC))

  - Alfred Joseph Oldham – b. 4 Aug 1888, bapt. 8 Aug 1888 (Baptism, **Rathmines Parish** (RC))

  - Evelyn Mary Oldham – b. 14 Aug 1891, bapt. 23 Aug 1891 (Baptism, **Rathmines Parish** (RC))

George Oldham (father):

Residence - 6 Hawthorn Terrace - August 14, 1878

1 St. Bridget Cottage, North Strand - August 2, 1880

57 Harold's Cross - August 8, 1888

8 Armstrong Street, Harold's Cross - August 23, 1891

- George St. John Oldham & Rebecca Oldham

Signature:

  - Henry Bewley Oldham – b. 30 May 1869, bapt. 18 Jul 1869 (Baptism, **Rathmines Parish**)

George St. John Oldham (father):

Residence - Drayton, Cambridge Road - July 18, 1869

Occupation - Medical Doctor - July 18, 1869

Hurst

- Gulielmo Oldham & Mary Anne Keogh
  - John Oldham – bapt. Jun 1806 (Baptism, **St. Nicholas Parish (RC)**)
  - Jane Oldham – bapt. 18 Oct 1807 (Baptism, **St. Nicholas Parish (RC)**)
- Henry Oldham & Mary Lane
  - Susan Oldham – bapt. 11 Nov 1837 (Baptism, **Murragh & Templemartin Parish (RC)**)
- Henry Oldham & Unknown
  - Arthur Oldham & Mary Spiers Stanley – 6 Jun 1878 (Marriage, **St. Stephen Parish**)

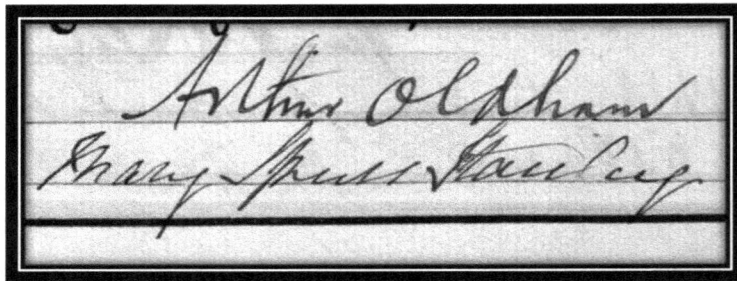

Signatures:

  ▪ Kathleen Oldham – b. 4 Jun 1879, bapt. 27 Jul 1879 (Baptism, **Leeson Park Parish**)

Arthur Oldham (son):

Residence - 19 Ailesbury Road, Booters Town - June 6, 1878

21 Elgin Road - July 27, 1879

Occupation - Solicitor - June 6, 1878

July 27, 1879

Mary Spiers Stanley, daughter of Robert Stanley (daughter-in-law):

Residence - 41 Mespil Road - June 6, 1878

Oldham Surname Ireland: 1600s to 1900s

Robert Stanley (father):

    Occupation - Merchant

Henry Oldham (father):

    Occupation - Solicitor

Wedding Witnesses:

Robert W. Stanley & Henry Oldham

Signatures:

- Hugh Oldham & Elizabeth Oldham – 3 Oct 1805 (Marriage, **St. Paul Parish**)

- Hugh Oldham & Mary Maguire – 2 Sep 1822 (Marriage, **St. James Parish**)

- James Oldham & Elizabeth Lacy

    o Gulielmo Oldham – b. 21 Oct 1860, bapt. 28 Oct 1860 (Baptism, **Rathmines Parish (RC)**)

James Oldham (father):

    Residence - Charlemont Street - October 28, 1860

Hurst

- James Oldham & Lucy Oldham

  - Lucy Mabel Oldham – b. 2 Jun 1871, bapt. 12 Jul 1871 (Baptism, **Rathmines Parish**)

James Oldham (father):

Residence - 10 Rostrevor Terrace - July 12, 1871

Occupation - Silk Weaver - July 12, 1871

- James Oldham & Mary Haig – 19 Mar 1833 (Marriage, **Taney Parish**)

James Oldham (husband):

Residence - Bellamoor Hall, Staffordshire - March 19, 1833

Mary Haig (wife):

Residence - Roebuck - March 19, 1833

Wedding Witnesses:

Robert Haig & John Haig

- James Oldham & Mary Oldham

  - Annette Mary Oldham – b. 29 Sep 1850, bapt. 13 Nov 1850 (Baptism, **St. Mary Parish**)

  - James William Massey Oldham – b. 11 Jul 1853, bapt. 10 Aug 1853 (Baptism, **St. Mary Parish**)

  - Frederick John Oldham – b. 24 Jun 1854, bapt. 19 Jul 1854 (Baptism, **St. Mary Parish**)

  - Mary Emily Oldham – b. 10 Oct 1855, bapt. 18 Nov 1855 (Baptism, **St. Mary Parish**)

James Oldham (father):

Residence - 84 Middle Abbey Street - November 13, 1850

Prince William Terrace Street - August 10, 1853

Oldham Surname Ireland: 1600s to 1900s

9 Prince William Terrace - July 19, 1854

November 18, 1855

Occupation - Wine Agent - November 13, 1850

Merchant - August 10, 1853

July 19, 1854

Wine Merchant - November 18, 1855

- James Oldham & Unknown
  - o Thomas Oldham – bur. 23 Oct 1711 (Burial, **St. Mary Parish**)

James Oldham (father):

Occupation - Tailor - October 23, 1711

- John Oldham & Amelia Unknown
  - o Elizabeth Anne Oldham – b. 8 Jan 1829, bapt. 25 Jan 1829 (Baptism, **St. Mark Parish**)
  - o Mary Anne Oldham – bapt. 15 Aug 1830 (Baptism, **St. Paul Parish**)
  - o Amelia Oldham – b. 15 Apr 1833, bapt. 26 May 1833 (Baptism, **St. James Parish**)

John Oldham (father):

Residence - 8 Great Brunswick Street - January 25, 1829

James Street - May 26, 1833

Occupation - Engraver - January 25, 1829

May 26, 1833

Hurst

- John Oldham & Elizabeth Fielding – 19 Nov 1780 (Marriage, **St. Bride Parish**)

John Oldham (husband):

Occupation - Shoemaker - November 19, 1780

- John Oldham & Elizabeth McCann
  - Mariah Oldham – bapt. 25 Jan 1844 (Baptism, **St. James Parish (RC)**)
- John Oldham & Elizabeth Unknown
  - Ellen Oldham – b. 29 Dec 1841, bapt. 24 Jan 1842 (Baptism, **St. James Parish**)

John Oldham (father):

Residence - Richmond - January 24, 1841

Occupation - Painter - January 24, 1841

- John Oldham & Judith Couban – 14 Oct 1804 (Marriage, **St. Peter Parish**)
- John Oldham & Mary Murphy
  - John Oldham – bapt. Sep 1832 (Baptism, **Rathmines Parish (RC)**)
- John Oldham & Mary Unknown
  - John Oldham – bapt. 22 Aug 1802 (Baptism, **St. Werburgh Parish**)
  - Anne Oldham – bapt. 3 Sep 1804 (Baptism, **St. Werburgh Parish**)

John Oldham (father):

Residence - Grafton Street - August 22, 1802

September 3, 1804

Oldham Surname Ireland: 1600s to 1900s

- John Oldham & Mary Unknown

  o Anne Oldham – bapt. 14 Dec 1819 (Baptism, **St. Mary, Pro Cathedral Parish** (RC))

John Oldham (father):

Residence - 45 Lower Liffy Street - December 14, 1819

- John Oldham & Mary Anne Hurley

  o Matthew Lawrence Oldham – b. 17 Aug 1894, bapt. 20 Aug 1894 (Baptism, **St. Mary, Pro Cathedral Parish** (RC))

John Oldham (father):

Residence - 5 upper Gloucester Street - August 20, 1894

- John Thomas Oldham & Louise Oldham

  o Bernice (B e r n i c e) Anne Louise Oldham – b. 12 Apr 1895, bapt. 8 Apr 1895 (Baptism, **Rotunda Chapel Parish**)

John Thomas Oldham (father):

Residence - 17 Richmond Cottages - April 8, 1895

Occupation - [Commercial] **Traveller - April 8, 1895**

Hurst

- Joseph Oldham & Christine Unknown

  o Margaret Miller Oldham – b. 10 Jun 1835, bapt. 24 Jun 1835 (Baptism, **St. Peter Parish**)

  o Joseph Oldham – b. 16 Nov 1836, bapt. 23 Dec 1836 (Baptism, **St. Peter Parish**)

  o Andrew Wingate Oldham – b. 18 Jul 1838, bapt. 21 Sep 1838 (Baptism, **St. Peter Parish**)

  o George Wingate Oldham – b. 8 Mar 1840, bapt. 5 Jun 1840 (Baptism, **St. Peter Parish**)

Signature:

Joseph Oldham (father):

Residence - No. 3 Herbert Place - June 24, 1835

September 21, 1838

Herbert Place - December 23, 1836

Robert Place - June 5, 1840

- Joshua Oldham & Jane Unknown

  o William Oldham – bapt. 4 Nov 1846 (Baptism, **SS. Michael & John Parish (RC)**)

- Marcus William Oldham & Jane Oldham

Signature:

  o Anne Mary Oldham – bapt. 9 Jul 1808 (Baptism, **St. Mary Parish**)

  o Marcus William Oldham & Jane Fairclough – 23 Apr 1851 (Marriage, **St. Peter Parish**)

Oldham Surname Ireland: 1600s to 1900s

Signature:

Signatures (Marriage):

- Margaret Frances Oldham – b. 12 Nov 1840, bapt. 10 Dec 1840 (Baptism, **St. Paul Parish**)

- Elizabeth Mary Oldham – b. 1 Nov 1842, bapt. 24 Nov 1842 (Baptism, **St. Paul Parish**)

- William Mark Oldham, b. 15 Feb 1844, bapt. 7 Apr 1844 (Baptism, **St. Paul Parish**) & Catherine Smith – 24 Jul 1885 (Marriage, **St. Peter Parish**)

Signatures:

William Mark Oldham (son):

Residence - 6 Ulverton Terrace, Dalkey - July 24, 1885

Occupation - Chemist - July 24, 1885

Catherine Smith, daughter of George Smith (daughter-in-law):

Residence - 8 Ormond Road, Rathmines - July 24, 1885

George Smith (father):

Occupation - Barrister

Marcus William Oldham (father):

Occupation - Gentleman

Wedding Witnesses:

Andrew Smith & George Bryan

Signatures:

- Mary Anne Oldham – b. 18 Feb 1852, bapt. 26 May 1852 (Baptism, **St. Peter Parish**)

- Elizabeth Margaret Oldham – b. 18 Dec 1854, bapt. 27 May 1855 (Baptism, **St. Peter Parish**)

Marcus William Oldham (son):

Residence - 31 Heytesbury Street - April 23, 1851

Queen Street - December 10, 1840

November 24, 1842

April 7, 1844

Oldham Surname Ireland: 1600s to 1900s

Longwood Avenue - May 26, 1852

No. 7 Bellville, Heytesbury Street - May 27, 1855

Occupation - Mercantile Clerk - April 23, 1851

May 26, 1852

May 27, 1855

Clerk in Bank of Ireland - December 10, 1840

Bank Clerk - November 24, 1842

Gentleman - April 7, 1844

Jane Fairclough, daughter of Evan Fairclough (daughter-in-law):

Residence - 39 George's Street - April 23, 1851

Evan Fairclough (father):

Occupation - Watchmaker

Marcus William Oldham (father):

Occupation - Attorney

Wedding Witnesses:

John Barrett & Isabella Barrett

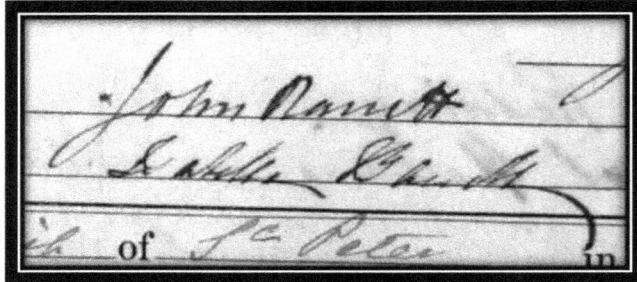

Signatures:

- Richard Oldham & Anastasia Nancy Bustead

  - Richard Oldham – bapt. 17 Jun 1821 (Baptism, **Ivelearly Parish** (RC))

  - John Oldham – bapt. 19 Jul 1823 (Baptism, **Ivelearly Parish** (RC))

  - Bridget Oldham – bapt. 22 Jan 1826 (Baptism, **Ivelearly Parish** (RC))

Richard Oldham (father):

Residence - Rossmore - June 17, 1821

July 19, 1823

January 22, 1826

- Richard Oldham & Anne Unknown

  - Margaret Oldham – bapt. 6 Feb 1855 (Baptism, **SS. Michael & John Parish** (RC))

- Richard Oldham & Julie Manning – 13 Feb 1866 (Marriage, **Kilmichael Parish** (RC))

Wedding Witnesses:

Timothy Manning & Daniel Oldham

Oldham Surname Ireland: 1600s to 1900s

- Robert Oldham & Catherine Connelly – 30 Nov 1779 (Marriage, **St. Mary Parish**)

- Robert Oldham & Jane Gallavan – 20 Feb 1814 (Marriage, **Bandon Parish** (RC))

Wedding Witnesses:

Philip Gallavan & Maurice Ahern

- Robert Oldham & Jane O'Donohue

  o Emily Oldham – b. 28 Oct 1878, bapt. 17 Nov 1878 (Baptism, **Rathmines Parish** (RC))

Robert Oldham (father):

Residence - Mt. Pleasant Avenue - November 17, 1878

- Robert Oldham & Mary Croly

  o Jean Oldham – bapt. 13 Aug 1821 (Baptism, **Kilbrittain Parish** (RC))

- Roland Oldham & Catherine Dillon

  o William Oldham – b. 1863, bapt. 1863 (Baptism, **Rathfarnham Parish** (RC))

Roland Oldham (father):

Residence - Rathfarnham - 1863

- Roland Oldham & Jane O'Donovan

  o Mary Josephine Oldham – b. 26 May 1874, bapt. 10 Jun 1874 (Baptism, **St. Mary, Pro Cathedral Parish** (RC))

Roland Oldham (father):

Residence - 26 Talbot Street - June 10, 1874

Hurst

- Roland Oldham & Jane Keating

  - Unknown Oldham – b. 7 Aug 1885, bapt. 14 Aug 1885 (Baptism, **St. Audoen Parish (RC)**)

Roland Oldham (father):

Residence - 53 High Street - August 14, 1885

- Samuel Oldham & Anne Curwen – 25 Feb 1813 (Marriage, **St. Andrew Parish**)

- Samuel Oldham & Anne Unknown

  - Anne Oldham, b. 28 Feb 1828, bapt. 16 Mar 1828 (Baptism, **St. Peter Parish**) & John Brinton – 13 Oct 1853 (Marriage, **St. Peter Parish**)

Signatures:

Anne Oldham (daughter):

Residence - Prince Arthur Terrace, Rathmines - October 13, 1853

John Brinton, son of Henry Brinton (son-in-law):

Residence - Kidder Master, Co. Worcester - October 13, 1853

Occupation - Merchant - October 13, 1853

Henry Brinton (father):

Occupation - Merchant

Samuel Oldham (father):

Occupation - Merchant

Wedding Witnesses:

Emily Jane Brinton & Samuel Oldham

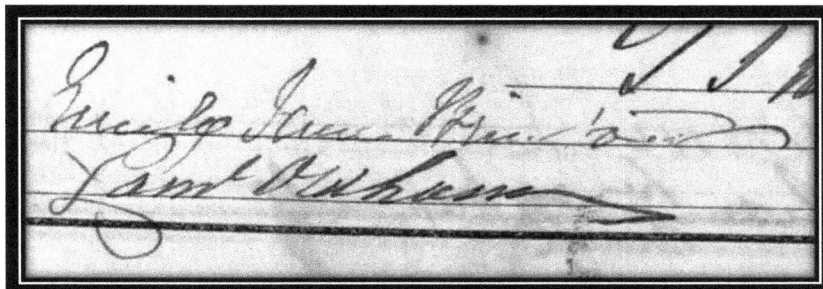

Signatures:

- o   James Oldham Oldham – b. 14 Mar 1830, bapt. 9 May 1830 (Baptism, **St. Peter Parish**)

Samuel Oldham (father):

Residence - Rathmines - 1828

Rathmines Church - May 9, 1830

- Samuel Oldham, bur. 13 Dec 1807 (Burial, **St. Peter Parish**) & Catherine Unknown

  o William Oldham – bapt. 21 Nov 1802 (Baptism, **St. Werburgh Parish**)

  o Jane Oldham – bapt. 23 Feb 1807 (Baptism, **St. Peter Parish**)

Samuel Oldham (father):

Residence - Bishop Street - November 21, 1802

February 23, 1807

before December 13, 1807

- Samuel Oldham & Unknown

  o Eldred Oldham & Anne Alker – 4 Apr 1846 (Marriage, **St. George Parish**)

Signature:

Signatures (Marriage):

  ▪ Alice Oldham – b. 24 Jun 1850, bapt. 6 Sep 1850 (Baptism, **St. Stephen Parish**)

Signature:

Oldham Surname Ireland: 1600s to 1900s

- Eldred Oldham, b. 4 Nov 1852, bapt. 24 Feb 1853 (Baptism, **St. Peter Parish**) & Elizabeth Mary Cooper – 26 Feb 1879 (Marriage, **St. George Parish**)

Signature:

Signatures (Marriage):

Eldred Oldham (son):

Residence - 57 Pembroke Road - February 26, 1879

Occupation - Merchant - February 26, 1879

Elizabeth Mary Cooper, daughter of James Cooper (daughter-in-law):

Residence - 101 Grafton Street - February 26, 1879

James Cooper (father):

Occupation - Esquire

Eldred Oldham (father):

Occupation - Merchant

Wedding Witnesses:

William Bolton, Charles Hubert Oldham, & M. Bolton

Hurst

Signatures:

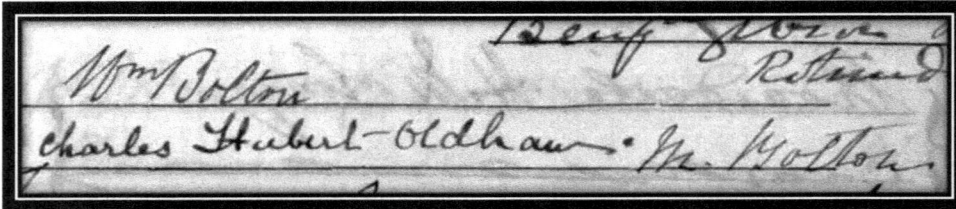

- Harold Oldham, b. 16 May 1854, bapt. 30 Aug 1854 (Baptism, **St. Peter Parish**) & Frances White

  - Eldred Matthew Oldham – b. 17 Aug 1879, bapt. 22 Aug 1879 (Baptism, **St. Mary, Haddington Road Parish (RC)**)

  - Helen Mary Oldham – b. 27 Jan 1880, bapt. 5 Feb 1881 (Baptism, **Rathmines Parish (RC)**)

  - Anne Ada Oldham – b. 27 May 1882, bapt. 3 Jun 1882 (Baptism, **St. Mary, Haddington Road Parish (RC)**)

  - Mary Frances Oldham – b. 17 Jul 1886, bapt. 26 Jul 1886 (Baptism, **St. Mary, Haddington Road Parish (RC)**)

  - Mabel Pauline Oldham – b. 29 Jun 1888, bapt. 11 Jul 1888 (Baptism, **St. Mary, Haddington Road Parish (RC)**)

Harold Oldham (son):

Residence - 84 Waterloo Road - August 22, 1879

Waterloo Road - February 5, 1881

54 Waterloo Road - June 3, 1882

July 26, 1886

July 11, 1888

Oldham Surname Ireland: 1600s to 1900s

- Anne Oldham & Thomas William Foster – 25 Jul 1882 (Marriage, **St. Stephen Parish**)

Signatures:

Anne Oldham (daughter):

    Residence - 17 Waterloo Road - July 25, 1882

Thomas William Foster, son of William Foster (son-in-law):

    Residence - 15 Wellington Road - July 25, 1882

    Occupation - Esquire - July 25, 1882

William Foster (father):

    Occupation - Bookseller

Eldred Oldham (father):

    Occupation - Merchant

Wedding Witnesses:

Eldred Oldham & Alice Oldham

Signatures:

Hurst

Eldred Oldham (son):

Residence - 12 Westmoreland Lane - April 4, 1846

15 Percy Place - September 6, 1850

No. 2 Wellington Terrace, Leinster Road - February 24, 1853

No. 1 Wellington Terrace, Rathmines - August 30, 1854

Occupation - Merchant - April 4, 1846

February 24, 1853

August 30, 1854

Linen Draper - September 6, 1850

Anne Alker, daughter of George Alker (daughter-in-law):

Residence - 3 Burnett Place - April 4, 1846

Occupation - Gentlewoman - April 4, 1846

George Alker (father):

Occupation - Gentleman

Samuel Oldham (father):

Occupation - Merchant

Oldham Surname Ireland: 1600s to 1900s

Wedding Witnesses:

George Alker & Samuel Oldham

Signatures:

- Samuel Baggot Oldham & Elizabeth Catherine Oldham

Signatures:

o Frances Louise Oldham & Herbert Thompson Stanley – 16 Apr 1879 (Marriage, **St. Stephen Parish**)

Signatures:

Frances Louise Oldham (daughter):

 Residence - 35 Upper Baggot Street - April 16, 1879

Herbert Thompson Stanley, son of Robert Stanley (son-in-law):

 Residence - Mespil Road - April 16, 1879

 Occupation - Wine Merchant - April 16, 1879

Robert Stanley (father):

 Occupation - Manufacturer

Samuel Baggot Oldham (father):

 Occupation - Esquire

Wedding Witnesses:

Samuel Baggot Oldham & L. F. Wayland

Signatures:

 o Florence Isabella Oldham, b. 11 Oct 1859, bapt. 6 Apr 1859 (Baptism, **St. Stephen Parish**) & Hugh Falconer Oldham – 25 Apr 1888 (Marriage, **St. Stephen Parish**)

Signatures:

Oldham Surname Ireland: 1600s to 1900s

Florence Isabella Oldham (daughter):

　　Residence - 35 Upper Baggot Street - April 25, 1888

Hugh Falconer Oldham, son of Thomas Oldham (son-in-law):

　　Residence - Monsall Newton Heath, Manchester - April 25, 1888

　　Occupation - Medical Doctor - April 25, 1888

Thomas Oldham (father):

　　Occupation - Director Geological Survey, India

Samuel Baggot Oldham (father):

　　Occupation - Esquire

Wedding Witnesses:

G. Fosters Oldham & Kathleen S. Oldham

Signatures:

o Margaret Blanche Oldham, b. 8 Oct 1860, bapt. 1 Mar 1861 (Baptism, **St. Stephen Parish**) & Leonard Kidd – 11 Apr 1889 (Marriage, **St. Stephen Parish**)

Signatures:

Margaret Blanche Oldham (daughter):

Residence - 58 Merrion Square - April 11, 1889

Leonard Kidd, son of Frederick William Kidd (son-in-law):

Residence - Carlton House, Enniskillen - April 11, 1889

Occupation - Medical Doctor - April 11, 1889

Frederick William Kidd (father):

Occupation - Esquire

Samuel Baggot Oldham (father):

Occupation - Esquire

Oldham Surname Ireland: 1600s to 1900s

Wedding Witnesses:

George H. Kidd & R. Glasgow Satteson

Signatures:

- Sarah Catherine Oldham – b. 20 Nov 1861, bapt. 21 Mar 1862 (Baptism, **St. Stephen Parish**)

- Emily Constance Oldham – b. 4 Nov 1865, bapt. 16 May 1866 (Baptism, **St. Peter Parish**)

Samuel Baggot Oldham (father):

Residence - 76 Upper Baggot Street - April 6, 1859

March 1, 1861

March 21, 1862

5 Upper Baggot Street - May 16, 1866

Occupation - Esquire - April 6, 1859

March 1, 1861

March 21, 1862

Gentleman - May 16, 1866

- Thomas Oldham & Catherine Unknown

    - William Oldham – bapt. 20 Feb 1778 (Baptism, **St. Michan Parish** (RC))

    - Mary Oldham – bapt. 20 Feb 1778 (Baptism, **St. Michan Parish** (RC))

Hurst

- Thomas Oldham & Harriet Oldham

    o John James Oldham – b. 3 Jan 1825, bapt. 5 Feb 1825 (Baptism, **St. Mark Parish**)

- Thomas Oldham & Henrietta Oldham

    o Emily Sarah Oldham – b. 29 Sep 1828, bapt. 12 Oct 1828 (Baptism, **St. George Parish**)

Thomas Oldham (father):

Residence - 2 Richmond Place - October 12, 1828

Occupation - Gentleman - October 12, 1828

- Thomas Oldham & Margaret Mahony

    o Matthew Oldham – bapt. 27 Feb 1837 (Baptism, **Murragh & Templemartin Parish** (RC))

    o John Oldham – bapt. 16 Jun 1841 (Baptism, **Murragh & Templemartin Parish** (RC))

- Thomas Oldham & Mary Oldham

    o Samuel Oldham – bapt. 1 Sep 1784 (Baptism, **St. Paul Parish**)

- Thomas Oldham & Mary Unknown

    o Sarah Oldham – bapt. 1751 (Baptism, **St. Andrew Parish** (RC))

- Thomas Oldham & Unknown

    o Thomas Oldham & Louisa Matilda Dixon – 17 Oct 1850 (Marriage, **St. Peter Parish**)

Signatures:

Oldham Surname Ireland: 1600s to 1900s

- Richard Dinon Oldham – b. 30 Jul 1858, bapt. 15 Sep 1858 (Baptism, **St. Stephen Parish**)

- Hugh Falconer Oldham & Florence Isabella Oldham – 25 Apr 1888 (Marriage, **St. Stephen Parish**)

Signatures:

Hugh Falconer Oldham (son):

   Residence - Monsall Newton Heath, Manchester - April **25, 1888**

   Occupation - Medical Doctor - April **25, 1888**

Florence Isabella Oldham, daughter of Samuel Baggot Oldham (daughter-in-law):

   Residence - **35** Upper Baggot Street - April **25, 1888**

Samuel Baggot Oldham (father):

   Occupation - Esquire

Thomas Oldham (father):

   Occupation - Director Geological Survey, India

Wedding Witnesses:

G. Fosters Oldham & Kathleen S. Oldham

Signatures:

Thomas Oldham (son):

    Residence - 18 Pembroke Road - October 17, 1850

        19 Pembroke Road - September 15, 1858

    Occupation - Esquire - October 17, 1850

        Director of Geological Survey in India - September 15, 1858

Louisa Matilda Dixon, daughter of William Dixon (daughter-in-law):

    Residence - 5 Herbert Place - October 17, 1850

William Dixon (father):

    Occupation - Merchant

Thomas Oldham (father):

    Occupation - Merchant

Wedding Witnesses:

George Folliott & Samuel Baggot Oldham

Signatures:

Oldham Surname Ireland: 1600s to 1900s

- Thomas Oldham & Unknown

  o Richard Oldham & Margaret Morton – 18 Jan 1860 (Marriage, **St. Thomas Parish**)

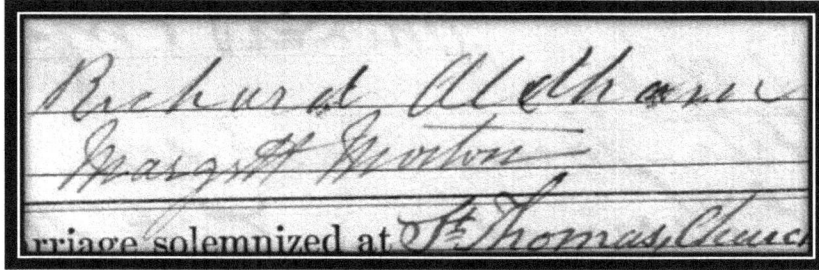

Signatures:

Richard Oldham (son):

   Residence - Nottingham Parade - January 18, 1860

   Occupation - Watchmaker - January 18, 1860

   Relationship Status at Marriage - widow

Margaret Morton, daughter of John Morton (daughter-in-law):

   Residence - Quinn's Place - January 18, 1860

John Morton (father):

   Occupation - Clerk

Thomas Oldham (father):

   Occupation - Clerk

Wedding Witnesses:

Mary Walsh & Bridget Purcell

Signatures:

- Thomas Oldham & Unknown
  - Charles Oldham & Elizabeth Kirwan – 30 Oct 1899 (Marriage, **Lucan Parish (RC)**)

Elizabeth Kirwan, daughter of Mark Kirwan (daughter-in-law):

Residence - Lucan - October 30, 1899

Wedding Witnesses:

Patrick Oldham & Catherine Kirwan

- Thomas Thomas Oldham & Mary Oldham
  - Thomas Thomas Oldham – bapt. 1842 (Baptism, **Palmerstown Parish (RC)**)
- Thomas Wilson Oldham & Mary Anne Bradley – 12 May 1831 (Marriage, **St. Mary Parish**)

Signatures:

Oldham Surname Ireland: 1600s to 1900s

o   Stanley Oldham & Anne Mary Bullen – 18 Oct 1864 (Marriage, **St. Anne Parish**)

Signatures:

- Edith Oldham – b. 20 Feb 1867, bapt. 27 Mar 1867 (Baptism, **St. Stephen Parish**)

- Arthur Clarks Oldham – b. 20 Feb 1868, bapt. 30 Apr 1868 (Baptism, **St. Stephen Parish**)

- Alfred Oldham – b. 13 Dec 1874, bapt. 14 Jul 1875 (Baptism, **St. Matthias Parish**)

Stanley Oldham (son):

Residence - 37 Grafton Street - October 18, 1864

Mespil Parade - March 27, 1867

25 Mespil Road - April 30, 1868

30 Mount Pleasant Square - July 14, 1875

Occupation - Merchant - October 18, 1864

Chemist - March 27, 1867

April 30, 1868

July 14, 1875

Anne Mary Bullen, daughter of Henry Adams Bullen (daughter-in-law):

Residence - 4 Wilton Terrace - October 18, 1864

Henry Adams Bullen (father):

    Occupation - Captain

Thomas Wilson Oldham (father):

    Occupation - Merchant

Wedding Witnesses:

James Beatty & William B. Oldham

Signatures:

Thomas Wilson Oldham (father):

    Residence - St. Anne Parish - May 12, 1831

Mary Anne Bradley (mother):

    Residence - St. Mary Parish - May 12, 1831

Wedding Witnesses:

John Figgis & Ray Bradley

Signatures:

Oldham Surname Ireland: 1600s to 1900s

- Unknown Oldham & Unknown

  o Arthur Robert Oldham

Signatures:

- Unknown Oldham & Unknown

  o Elizabeth Oldham

Signature:

- Unknown Oldham & Unknown

  o Emily Oldham & Edmund Brewer Munro – 1 Jun 1861 (Marriage, **St. Peter Parish**)

Signatures:

Hurst

Emily Oldham (daughter):

    Residence - 104 Wynnefield Place, Upper Rathmines - June 1, 1861

Edmund Brewer Munro, son of Henry Loftus Munro (son-in-law):

    Residence - 56 Peter Street, Northampton - June 1, 1861

    Occupation - Civil Engineer - June 1, 1861

    Relationship Status at Marriage - widow

Henry Loftus Munro (father):

    Occupation - Surveying Engineer

Unknown Oldham (father):

    Occupation - Officer in the Bank of England

Wedding Witnesses:

H. Hanlon & George A. Hanlon

Signatures:

- Unknown Oldham & Unknown

  o James Oldham

Signature:

- Unknown Oldham & Unknown

  o James Oldham

Signature:

- Unknown Oldham & Unknown

  o John J. Oldham

Signature:

- Unknown Oldham & Unknown

  o Margaret F. Oldham

Signature:

- Unknown Oldham & Unknown

  o Mary J. Oldham

Signature:

- Unknown Oldham & Unknown

  o Unknown Oldham, d. bef. 6 Sep 1873 & Emily Bradshaw

  o Emily Bradshaw Oldham (2nd Marriage) & Vincent De Lisle – 6 Sep 1873 (Marriage, **St. Stephen Parish**)

Signatures:

Emily Bradshaw, daughter of Robert Bradshaw (daughter-in-law):

  Residence - 37 Sandycove Terrace, Kingstown - September 6, 1873

  Relationship Status at 2nd Marriage - widow

Vincent de Lisle, son of Francis De Lisle (son-in-law):

  Residence - 44 Lower Mount Street - September 6, 1873

  Occupation - Esquire - September 6, 1873

Francis De Lisle (father):

    Occupation - Land Agent

Robert Bradshaw (father):

    Occupation - Merchant

Wedding Witnesses:

Samuel De Lisle & Robert Bradshaw

Signatures:

- Unknown Oldham & Unknown

    o William Oldham

Signature:

- Unknown Oldham & Unknown

  o William Oldham

Signature:

- William Oldham & Anne Keogh – 28 Jul 1805 (Marriage, **St. Paul Parish**)

- William Oldham & Catherine Unknown

  o Agnes Oldham – bapt. Oct 1834 (Baptism, **SS. Michael & John Parish (RC)**)

- William Oldham & Jane Unknown

  o Anne Oldham – bapt. 1842 (Baptism, **St. Andrew Parish (RC)**)

- William Oldham & Margaret Coghlan – 16 Feb 1828 (Marriage, **Bandon Parish (RC)**)

Wedding Witnesses:

James Coghlan & Julie Hart

- William Oldham & Margaret Sullivan

  o Margaret Oldham – bapt. 22 Oct 1819 (Baptism, **Kilmurry Parish (RC)**)

- William Oldham & Mary Anne Unknown

  o Thomas Oldham – b. 1811, bapt. 1811 (Baptism, **Rathfarnham Parish (RC)**)

  o Mary Oldham – b. 1813, bapt. 1813 (Baptism, **Rathfarnham Parish (RC)**)

  o George Oldham – b. 1815, bapt. 1815 (Baptism, **Rathfarnham Parish (RC)**)

  o Henry Oldham – b. 1817, bapt. 1817 (Baptism, **Rathfarnham Parish (RC)**)

  o Charlotte Oldham – b. 1821, bapt. 1821 (Baptism, **Rathfarnham Parish (RC)**)

Oldham Surname Ireland: 1600s to 1900s

- William Oldham & Sarah Elizabeth Carmichael (C a r m i c h a e l) – 14 Apr 1835 (Marriage, **St. Peter Parish**)

William Oldham (husband):

Residence - 7 French Street - April 14, 1835

Sarah Elizabeth Carmichael (wife):

Residence - French Street - April 14, 1835

Wedding Witnesses:

James Carmichael & Thomas Pickering

- William Oldham & Unknown
  - Margaret Frances Oldham & George Eldon Coates – 27 May 1885 (Marriage, **St. Matthias Parish**)

Signatures:

Margaret Frances Oldham (daughter):

Residence - 9 Charlemont Place - May 27, 1885

George Eldon Coates, son of William Coates (son-in-law):

Residence - Abbeyview Abbeyslemle, Co. Longford - May 27, 1885

Occupation - Gentleman - May 27, 1885

Relationship Status at Marriage - widow

Hurst

William Coates (father):

Occupation - Gentleman

William Oldham (father):

Occupation - Gentleman

Wedding Witnesses:

George Bryan & Catherine Smith

Signatures:

- William Field Oldham & Unknown
    - William Joseph Oldham & Frances Warren – 26 Jun 1849 (Marriage, **St. Peter Parish**)

Signatures:

William Joseph Oldham (son):

Residence - Ship Street Barracks - June 26, 1849

Occupation - Captain, 2nd Queen's Regiment - June 26, 1849

Oldham Surname Ireland: 1600s to 1900s

Frances Warren, daughter of Richard Warren (daughter-in-law):

    Residence - 29 Upper Mount Street - June 26, 1849

Richard Warren (father):

    Occupation - Medical Doctor

William Field Oldham (father):

    Occupation - Major in the Army

Wedding Witnesses:

John Edward Herrick & Daniel Conner

Signatures:

Individual Baptisms/Births

None Were Listed

Individual Burials

- Catherine Oldham – b. 1762, bur. 20 Dec 1849 (Burial, **St. Peter Parish**)

Catherine Oldham (deceased):

   Residence - Arbour Hill - before December 20, 1849

   Age at Death - 87 years

- Charles Oldham – b. Feb 1849, bur. 22 Aug 1849 (Burial, **St. Peter Parish**)

Charles Oldham (deceased):

   Residence - Grant's Row - before August 22, 1849

   Age at Death - 7 months

- Elizabeth Oldham – bur. 10 Aug 1831 (Burial, **St. Paul Parish**)
- Elizabeth Oldham – b. 1814, bur. 15 Jan 1839 (Burial, **St. Paul Parish**)

Elizabeth Oldham (deceased):

   Age at Death - 25 years

- Ellen Oldham – b. Sep 1826, bur. 3 Mar 1827 (Burial, **St. Nicholas Without Parish**)

Ellen Oldham (deceased):

   Residence - Francis Street - before March 3, 1827

   Age at Death - 7 months

Hurst

- Ellen Oldham – bur. 7 Mar 1827 (Burial, **St. Nicholas Without Parish**)

Ellen Oldham (deceased):

 Residence - Francis Street - before March 7, 1827

- George Oldham – b. 1782, bur. 4 May 1837 (Burial, **St. Mary Parish**)

George Oldham (deceased):

 Residence - Simpson's Hospital - before May 4, 1837

 Age at Death - 55 years

- Herbert N. Oldham – b. 1826, bur. 13 Feb 1847 (Burial, **St. Paul Parish**)

Herbert N. Oldham (deceased):

 Residence - Suffolk Street - before February 13, 1847

 Age at Death - 21 years

- John Oldham – bur. 16 Jan 1809 (Burial, **St. Paul Parish**)
- John Oldham – bur. 26 Nov 1811 (Burial, **St. Paul Parish**)
- Margaret Oldham – b. 1783, bur. 17 Apr 1855 (Burial, **St. Paul Parish**)

Margaret Oldham (deceased):

 Residence - Pembroke Road - before April 17, 1855

 Age at Death - 72 years

- Mary Oldham – bur. 7 Feb 1809 (Burial, **St. Paul Parish**)
- Mary Oldham – bur. 24 Jun 1811 (Burial, **St. Paul Parish**)

Oldham Surname Ireland: 1600s to 1900s

- Mary Oldham – bur. 6 Jun 1813 (Burial, **St. Paul Parish**)

- Peter Oldham – bur. 6 Jul 1671 (Burial, **St. Peter Parish**)

Peter Oldham (deceased):

　Residence - St. Stephen's Green - before July 6, 1671

- Samuel Oldham – b. 1793, d. 23 Aug 1815, bur. 1815 (Burial, **St. Peter Parish**)

Samuel Oldham (deceased):

　Age at Death - 22 years

- Sarah Oldham – b. 1805, bur. 15 Oct 1842 (Burial, **St. Paul Parish**)

Sarah Oldham (deceased):

　Residence - Suffolk Street - before October 15, 1842

　Age at Death - 37 years

- Thomas Oldham – bur. 31 Jan 1787 (Burial, **St. Paul Parish**)

- Thomas Oldham – b. 1771, bur. 27 Feb 1834 (Burial, **St. Paul Parish**)

Thomas Oldham (deceased):

　Age at Death - 63 years

Individual Marriages

- Catherine Oldham & Dionysius Sheehan

  o Anne Sheehan – b. 1900, bapt. 1900 (Baptism, **Lucan Parish (RC)**)

Dionysius Sheehan (father):

Residence - Woodville - 1900

- Catherine Oldham & John Hart

  o Mary Anne Hart – b. 23 Jun 1880, bapt. 28 Jun 1880 (Baptism, **St. Nicholas Parish** (RC))

John Hart (father):

Residence - 72 Bride Street - June 28, 1880

- Catherine Oldham & Thomas Wall – 5 Jul 1784 (Marriage, **St. Audoen Parish**)

Wedding Witnesses:

Nicholas Wale & William Wale

- Charlotte Frances Oldham & Henry Charles Hanlon – 4 Sep 1848 (Marriage, **Rathfarnham Parish (RC)**)

  o Charles William Hanlon – bapt. 2 Mar 1851 (Baptism, **Rathmines Parish** (RC))

  o Charles Gulielmo Hanlon – bapt. 2 Mar 1851 (Baptism, **Rathmines Parish** (RC))

  o Charlotte Mary Anne Hanlon – bapt. 11 Dec 1852 (Baptism, **Rathmines Parish** (RC))

  o Jane Harriet Hanlon – bapt. 23 Jul 1854 (Baptism, **Rathmines Parish** (RC))

  o Frances Mary Hanlon – b. 3 Jan 1857, bapt. 16 Jan 1857 (Baptism, **Rathmines Parish** (RC))

- Josephine Hanlon – b. 29 Mar 1858, bapt. 16 Jun 1858 (Baptism, **Rathmines Parish** (RC))

- Edward Hanlon – b. 3 Nov 1860, bapt. 11 Jan 1861 (Baptism, **Rathmines Parish** (RC))

- Henry G. J. Hanlon – b. 14 Jun 1863, bapt. 7 Aug 1863 (Baptism, **Rathmines Parish** (RC))

Henry Charles Hanlon (father):

Residence - Belville, Rathgar Road - June 16, 1858

Rathmines - January 11, 1861

August 7, 1863

Wedding Witnesses:

William Oldham & Mary Oldham

- Elizabeth Oldham & Andrew Ledsam – 5 Aug 1780 (Marriage, **St. Audoen Parish**)
- Elizabeth Oldham & Edward Jones – 28 Apr 1840 (Marriage, **St. Peter Parish**)

Elizabeth Oldham (wife):

Residence - Herbert Place - April 28, 1840

Edward Jones (husband):

Residence - Roundtown, Rathfarnham - April 28, 1840

Wedding Witnesses:

J. W. Oldham & James Oldham

- Elizabeth Oldham & James Nicholson – 15 Jan 1786 (Marriage, **St. Paul Parish**)
- Elizabeth Oldham & John Ryan
  - John Joseph Ryan – b. 1900, bapt. 1900 (Baptism, **St. Andrew Parish** (RC))

Hurst

John Ryan (father):

Residence - 37 South King's Street - 1900

- Elizabeth Oldham & William Robinson – 26 Sep 1803 (Marriage, **St. Peter Parish**)

- Ellen Oldham & John Martin

  o Mary Ellen Martin – b. 24 Apr 1896, bapt. 14 Sep 1896 (Baptism, **SS. Michael & John Parish** (RC))

John Martin (father):

Residence - Lower Castle Yard - September 14, 1896

- Frances Oldham & Alexander Stewart – 15 Sep 1770 (Marriage, **St. Audoen Parish**)

- Henrietta Oldham & William Mapplyn – 21 May 1847 (Marriage, **Rathfarnham Parish** (RC))

Wedding Witnesses:

Patrick Waldham & Charlotte Oldham

- Jane Charlotte Oldham & James Hanlon

  o Roseanne Ida Hanlon – bapt. 26 Aug 1839 (Baptism, **Rathmines Parish** (RC))

  o Charlotte Flora Hanlon – b. 1840 bapt. Dec 1840 (Baptism, **Rathfarnham Parish** (RC)) (Baptism, **Rathmines Parish** (RC))

  o George Oldham Hanlon – b. 1842, bapt. 1842 (Baptism, **Rathfarnham Parish** (RC))

  o Henry Oldham Hanlon – b. 1844, bapt. 1844 (Baptism, **Rathfarnham Parish** (RC))

  o Henrietta Hanlon – bapt. Apr 1846 (Baptism, **Rathmines Parish** (RC))

  o Arthur Oldham Hanlon – bapt. 20 Nov 1848 (Baptism, **Rathmines Parish** (RC))

  o Helen Jane Hanlon – bapt. 13 Jul 1850 (Baptism, **Rathmines Parish** (RC))

  o Caroline Ada Thomasina Hanlon – bapt. 17 May 1855 (Baptism, **Rathmines Parish** (RC))

Oldham Surname Ireland: 1600s to 1900s

- Jane Oldham & John Crowly – 4 Feb 1838 (Marriage, **Bandon Parish (RC)**)

Wedding Witnesses:

Richard Ahern & Michael Oldham

- Jane Oldham & Timothy Crean

  ○ Judith Crean – bapt. 16 Sep 1826 (Baptism, **Kilmichael Parish (RC)**)

Timothy Crean (father):

Residence - Knockane - September 16, 1826

- Jane Oldham & William Haly

  ○ Catherine Haly – bapt. 23 Jan 1829 (Baptism, **Kilmichael Parish (RC)**)

- Jenny Oldham & Timothy Currian

  ○ Eleanor Currian – bapt. 22 Jul 1821 (Baptism, **Kilmichael Parish (RC)**)

  ○ Judith Currian – bapt. 15 Jun 1823 (Baptism, **Kilmichael Parish (RC)**)

- Julie Oldham & John Flinn

  ○ Elizabeth Flinn – b. 21 Nov 1871, bapt. 24 Nov 1871 (Baptism, **St. Nicholas Parish (RC)**)

John Flinn (father):

Residence - 50 New Street - November 24, 1871

- Margaret Oldham & Gulielmo Henry Barry

  ○ Mary J. Barry – bapt. 27 Sep 1879 (Baptism, **Rathmines Parish (RC)**)

- Mary Oldham & George Byrne (B y r n e) – 4 Jun 1841 (Marriage, **St. Peter Parish**)

Mary Oldham (wife):

Residence - Shinrone - June 4, 1841

Hurst

George Byrne (husband):

Residence - Shinrone, King's County - June 4, 1841

Occupation - Farmer - June 4, 1841

Wedding Witnesses:

William Oldham & John Oldham

- Mary Oldham & Henry Wilkins – 20 Jul 1805 (Marriage, **St. Paul Parish**)

- Mary Oldham & Joseph McEllicott – 5 Sep 1849 (Marriage, **Rathfarnham Parish (RC)**)

Wedding Witnesses:

William Oldham & Edward Oldham

- Mary Oldham & Michael Cronin

  o Daniel Cronin – bapt. 26 Feb 1856 (Baptism, **Cork -South Parish (RC)**)

  o Margaret Cronin – bapt. 9 May 1858 (Baptism, **Cork -South Parish (RC)**)

  o John Cronin – bapt. 31 Jul 1860 (Baptism, **Cork -South Parish (RC)**)

- Mary Anne Oldham & Malachi Dunn

  o William Dunn – bapt. 1774 (Baptism, **SS. Michael & John Parish (RC)**)

- Rebecca Oldham & John Henry Byrne (B y r n e) – 19 Oct 1844 (Marriage, **St. Peter Parish**)

Rebecca Oldham (wife):

Residence - Charlemont Street - October 19, 1844

Occupation - Spinster - October 19, 1844

Oldham Surname Ireland: 1600s to 1900s

John Henry Byrne (husband):

Residence - York Street - October 19, 1844

Wedding Witnesses:

John Oldham & Anne Jane Byrne

- Sarah Oldham & Henry Brooks

    o Catherine Brooks – bapt. 29 May 1791 (Baptism, **St. Michan Parish** (RC))

    o Patrick Brooks – bapt. 21 Feb 1793 (Baptism, **St. Michan Parish** (RC))

- Teresa Oldham & John Quinn

    o Michael Quinn & Anne Martin – 4 Jul 1880 (Marriage, **Rathmines Parish** (RC))

Michael Quinn (son):

Residence - Windsor Terrace - July 4, 1880

Anne Martin, daughter of Patrick Martin & Mary Francy (daughter-in-law):

Residence - Leeson Park - July 4, 1880

Wedding Witnesses:

Jane Murphy & Catherine Quinn

- Teresa Oldham & Thomas Brazil

    o Veronica Mary Brazil – b. 21 Nov 1903, bapt. 29 Nov 1903 (Baptism, **Rathmines Parish** (RC))

Thomas Brazil (father):

Residence - 7 Levier Street, Harold's Cross - November 29, 1903

Name Variations

Includes Latin and Abbreviated forms of names found in the original documents.

Abigail = Abigale, Abigall

Anne = Ann, Anna, Annae

Bartholomew = Barth, Bartholmeus, Bartholomeo

Bridget = Birgis, Brigid, Brigida, Bridgit

Catherine = Catharine, Catharina, Catharinae, Catherina, Cath, Catha, Cathae, Cathe, Cathn, Kate

Charles = Carolus, Charls, Chas

Christopher = Christoph

Daniel = Danielem, Danielis

Edmund = Edmond

Edward = Ed, Edwd

Eleanor = Eleo, Eleonora, Elinor, Ellenor

Elizabeth = Betty, Elisa, Elisabeth, Eliz, Eliza, Elizab, Elizh, Elizth

Ellen = Elena, Ellena

Emily = Emilia

Esther = Essie, Ester

Francis = Fransicum

George = Geo, Georg, Georgius

Grace = Gratiae

Gulielmo = Guil, Guillelmi, Gulielmum, Guillelmus, Gulmi

Helen = Helena

Oldham Surname Ireland: 1600s to 1900s

Honor = Hanora, Honora

James = Jacobi, Jacobus, Jas

Jane = Joanna

Jeanne = Jeannae, Joannae

Joan = Johanna, Joney

John = Jno, Joannem, Joannes, Johannis

Joseph = Jos

Juliana = Julian

Leticia = Letitia, Lettice, Letticia

Lewis = Louis

Luke = Lucas

Margaret = Margarita, Margaritae, Margeret, Marget, Margt

Martha = Marthae

Mary = Maria, My

Mary Anne = Marianna, Marianne, Maryanne

Michael = Michaelis, Michl

Patrick = Pat, Patt, Patk, Patricii, Patricius

Peter = Petri

Richard = Ricardi, Ricardus, Rich, Richd

Robert = Roberti

Rose = Rosa, Rosae

Thomas = Thom, Thomae, Thoms, Thos, Ths

Timothy = Timotheus, Timy

William = Wil, Will, Willm, Wm

Notes

Notes

Notes

Notes

Notes

Notes

Index

Oldham Surname Ireland: 1600s to 1900s

L

M

N

O

Hurst

Oldham Surname Ireland: 1600s to 1900s

Hurst

Quinn Families

About The Author

Donovan Hurst graduated from San Diego State University with a Bachelor of Arts in the major field of studies of History and a minor in the field of studies of Anthropology. He is a current member of The General Society of Mayflower Descendants and has been conducting genealogical research for over 10 years tracing back his ancestors to their ancestral homelands in Denmark, England, France, Germany, Ireland, Norway, and Scotland.